The King
is a Fink

Brant Parker and
Johnny Hart

CORONET BOOKS
Hodder Fawcett

Coronet edition 1972
Fifth impression 1981

Printed and bound in Great Britain for
Hodder and Stoughton Paperbacks,
a division of Hodder and Stoughton Ltd,
Mill Road, Dunton Green, Sevenoaks, Kent
(Editorial Office: 47 Bedford Square, London WC1 3DP)
by Hunt Barnard Printing Ltd,
Aylesbury, Bucks

ISBN 0 340 15816 6

EUREKA!... I'VE FOUND IT!

...A MATERIAL STRONGER THAN ARMOR.

WHAT IS IT?

CRABGRASS.

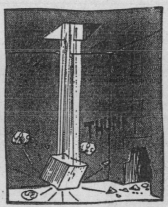

SIRE, THERE IS A KNIGHT AT THE GATE RECRUITING AN ARMY FOR A CRUSADE.

WHO ARE THEY CRUSADING AGAINST?

THE TURKS, SIRE

TELL HIM I CAN'T SPARE ANY MEN.

NOW, ADAMAZUK, ABOUT THOSE DANCING GIRLS YOU WERE TALKING ABOUT.

3

YOU MUST BE KIDDING.

HOW CAN YOU SLIP ON A CARROT?

I HAD NO CHOICE. BANANAS ARE OUT OF SEASON.

YOU'VE FAILED IN EVERY MISSION YOU'VE ATTEMPTED...

...GIVE ME ONE GOOD REASON WHY I SHOULDN'T HAVE YOUR HEAD!

YOUR CROWN WOULD BE HANGING DOWN AROUND YOUR EYES.

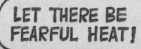

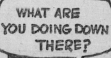

5

HEY, TURNKEY! HOW COME THEY CALL THE KING'S CHAIR A THRONE?

'CAUSE EVERY TIME YOU WALK UP TO IT YOU GET THRONE IN THE DUNGEON ... HAW HAR HEE HOO HOO ...

KAZANG

WIZ, I NEED SOMETHING TO MAKE ME BRAVE, FEARLESS AND COURAGEOUS.

KA ZAN G!

HOW CAN YOU LIVE IN SUCH SQUALOR, BUNG?

I HAVE TO, WIZ — I WAS BANISHED HERE BY THE KING FOR AN INEPT PERFORMANCE.

WHAT'S IN ALL THOSE BARRELS?

WINE.

HAPPINESS IS A THING CALLED "BANISHMENT."

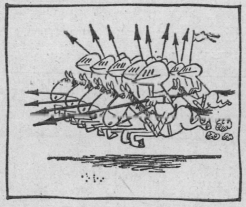

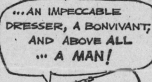

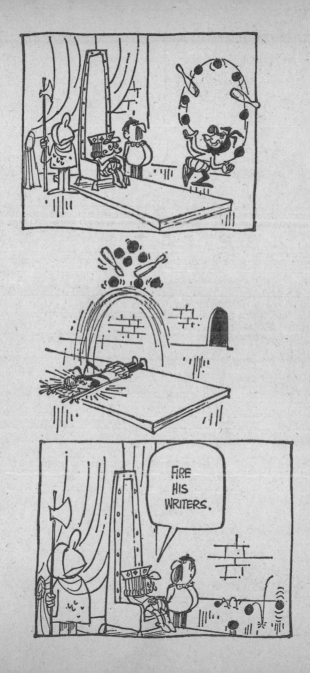

FAREWELL, BRAVE, FEARLESS, GALLANT SIR RODNEY.

THERE IS NOTHING QUITE AS SORROWFUL AS THE CRY OF A WOUNDED DRAGON.

AAARRGGHH

HAIL! SIR RODNEY!

WHAT HAVE YOU GOT FOR THIS THROAT, WIZ? THESE AAARRGHHS ARE KILLING ME.

8

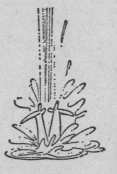